The Importance of Fatherhood

The Importance of
Fatherhood

Life Experiences and Advice to Help You
Navigate Through Fatherhood

Saquan Minor

Contents

Introduction

Every day we wake up and live life. I think we all could agree that life can be very
Hard and harsh at times. Life can also be loving and exciting at times. Whether
Ending the day in joy, sadness, anger or pain. How we spread our love plays the
Most dominant role in our lives in my opinion. This book contains information
That gives insight and guidance to those who are thinking about becoming a new
To already existing, and anyone willing to listen and maybe learn about Saquan
Minor experience of becoming, being and existing, as well as what Saquan has
Learn about being not just a father but a single loving father. Saquan writes
About when fatherhood begins, the importance of balancing fatherhood, making

A father's sacrifice, transferring and understanding information from father to father,
A father's role in life, and your vessel being the source of creation as a father.
Also, giving you insight into what type of environment Saquan comes from.
Help you better understand more of the battles Saquan faced as well as an
Inspiration and motivation for those in similar or worse positions being a father
Starting with before fatherhood.

Chapter 1
Before Fatherhood

In my younger days, I was raised in a low-income area living in Durham, North Carolina. It is often common to see children without a father. Naturally growing up in a survival state of mind because of the conditions and environments they are raised in. Where crime is a way of life and a way to maintain or gain whatever it is that a child loves. My mother did the best she could do as far as keeping our lives together given the circumstances. Mom was not perfect, but I love my mother and I appreciate everything she taught me. As a child we do not understand the reasoning parents do what they do or the choices they make and how it affects us. The life she chose to live shaped me into the young man you are getting to know and understand as you continue to read. My father did not come around until I was about eleven or twelve years old. By that time, I was full of anger and disappointment. From dealing so much with my mom and not having a positive male role model to creating order inside our home. My oldest brother was a young man searching for himself. Always working toward building a solid foundation we could stand on without falling. Still,there was only so much my brother could do at that time. No matter what happened to us, my brother was there for me. I am very thankful for everything he has shown and contributed to me and the man I am today. I am honored to call him my brother and proud of the man he has grown to become. My brother moved out when I was eight years old. From that point it was my mom and me. Her way of surviving was creating a place or spot to hustle or gamble where everyone could come and make money. From the trappers to the boosters and the robbers to the whores. The spot was a place where there is no judgement on character. The only thing that matters is that your money is green. As a child I was always excited to see the entertainment the adults would bring. Every other day I could count on there being a party and seeing them wild out enjoying the amusement. There was no need for television while they were around. I had a live action filled show in my living room. Being a child and growing up in that type of environment, I was able to soak up a lot of information at a very young age being around them. So much was happening all the time at one time I did not even think about asking where my father was anymore. My mother would bring me humongous stacks of cash to my bedroom and tell me to hide it. As soon as she walks out of the room, I count the money. While my fingers swipe and my brain counts, I cannot help but think about how I can make my own money. I noticed that adults would always drink and smoke, having soda and chips but no food. That is when it dawned on me to sell plates. I boiled packs of hotdogs, made chili, fried French fries, and sold guest plates for five dollars apiece. It was at that moment that I became a young entrepreneur. Everyone was astonished that I figured out how to make money for myself at such a young age. The parties were always late nights, so I would use my school time to catch up on sleep. I never felt like I was an actual kid because I was always around adults. Even though I was focused on getting money. Deep down inside my soul I felt abandoned. My father was not there, and my mom was in her own world leaving me to fend for myself. As I got older, I found my own ways of masking the pain. Basically, I was living life to the fullest doing whatever I wanted. Nothing but parties, smoking, drinking, and having sex with all type of women. I was riding till the wheels fell off. That was my way of relieving my frustration and having total control over situations. Then I took my hustle to the next level by selling drugs while working a nine to five job. I was infatuated with money. Cash, change, check, or credit exchange, I would take it any way I could get it and do just about anything for it. I did not even consider having children at that time. I was twenty years old and the last thing on my mind was having a child. Then "ring," I got a phone call that changed my life forever saying that my girlfriend at that time was pregnant. Growing up without a father can cause emotional and social difficulties that can affect the well-being and development of a child. Fatherless children are at a higher risk of experiencing negative outcomes such as depression, anxiety, low self-esteem, substance abuse, and behavioral problems. For you who are just now thinking about having a child or having a child, but that child is not here yet, have a child or being a father figure in a child's life that is not your biological child and carry some of these same traits from your childhood that may cause a problem when raising a child. The following information may help you in your journey of being a father. Fathers contribute to the overall well-being of their families by sharing responsibilities like household chores, caregiving, and financial support. Fathers who are engaged and involved in their children's lives also have lower rates of depression, and higher life satisfaction. Therefore, fatherhood is truly essential for the development and growth of children, families, and societies. Father involvement is important for a child's emotional development and overall well-being. Fathers provide guidance, support, and role modeling that help children to navigate the challenges of life. Fatherly involvement can also help children improve their academic performance, develop stronger social skills, and build healthier relationships. Be sure to provide emotional and financial support. Providing emotional support to a child helps develop positive self-esteem and confidence. Providing financial support ensures your child's basic needs are met. Be a great example to your kids. Show what qualities a role model should put forth even if you are not exactly who they want to be like when they grow up. Being a role model as a father can be very impactful when it comes to their daughters and especially their sons. Demonstrating first or after being misguided respect, health, positive behavior, values, responsibility, citizenship, and any other morals has a significant impact on children's lives. Help promote your child's academic success by encouraging and supporting their learning abilities and educational growth. No matter how small it is. Give them big praise for maximum results later in life. However, it is important to note that not all children have fathers or have positive relationships with their fathers. Other family members, friends, mentors, or community members can help provide the support and guidance that a father might otherwise provide. Fatherhood plays a crucial part in every family and childhood life. Some-things are needed from fathers like boundaries that are not meant to be cross, discipline, sternness, emotional support or learn how to deal with emotional detachments from all relationships whether business or personal. Fatherhood also could help with mental or physical protection and strength in areas that may not be able to be provided from your significant others, because they do not carry the wisdom or positive counseling you have been graced with through life's experiences only a father could encounter. If you or someone you know is a father-less child or concerned about the impact of fatherlessness on a child. In my opinion, it is important to seek guidance and support from a professional, such as counselors, ther-apists, or social workers. These professionals can help children and families to deal with emotional and social challenges of fatherlessness and work towards building a brighter future. Whether before or after fatherhood begins.

Chapter 2
Fatherhood Begins

First and foremost, I would like to start this chapter by saying, "Congratulations to all new fathers!". This must be a very exciting time in your life. I know it was for me. The beginning stage can be very challenging at times, seeing how most of the world's advice differs when it comes to raising a child and no one wants to be told what to do with their own child. My goal is not to tell you how to raise your child. My goal is to give you all the tips and advice I can on what helped me the most as a father and parent. If you feel like it correlates to you feel free to try it. Consider me as a helpful assistant navigating you through this new stage of your life. The first thing I would tell you as a new father is get plenty of rest. Being a new father can be exhausting. It is important to prioritize sleep whenever you can in your schedule. Take turns with your partner caring for the baby at night. That way both of you can get some rest or if you are by yourself, sleep when the baby is asleep, just make sure the baby is safely positioned free from anything that could harm the baby. Second, I would advise you to ask for help. Do not be afraid to ask genuine family and friends for help with things like meal prep, cleaning, or running errands. They would more than likely be willing to lend a helping hand. Third, bond with your baby. Spend all the quality time you can with your baby through activities like reading, singing, or just cuddling. This can help strengthen your connection and create a sense of security and comfort for your little one. Fourth, take care of yourself. It is important to prioritize your own self-care even as you care for your new baby. Love on yourself. Make time for hobbies, exercise, and socializing to help maintain your own well-being. Without loving yourself first there is no way possible you can love your little one or anyone properly. Fifth, be patient with yourself and your little one. Adjusting to life with a new baby can be challenging. Take things one day at a time and remember that it is ok ask for help when you need it. I hope this advice helps you on your journey through fatherhood. My journey into fatherhood began on May 7th, 2010. On that day I met my first-born son Jayln. Jayln birth is one of the most amazing moments of my life. Lol. I felt fear, happiness, excitement, and nervousness all at the same time. My emotions were all over the place. When they handed him to me, I held his little body. All I thought to myself was, wow, I am a dad. Looking into his little eyes something touched my spirit that day. I just knew that I had to become a real man for my son. Growing up without my father and a not having many male role models in my life. I knew this was not going to be an easy task. The first few weeks were not too bad, I made sure I was with his mom as much as possible when I did not have to work, to remove some of the stress off of her. Late nights and early mourning's were the toughest. Jayln's mother and I would take turns making bottles, changing diapers at all types of crazy hours aiming our best to get him on a tight schedule. Even though I was a father. I was still young and making mistakes. While still learning how to be a man. I was still involved in the streets. Making moves to the money and sleeping around with other women did not automatically stop. I was addicted to the lifestyle. I was living life to the fullest in my eyes. Jayln's mother and I separated when Jayln was around three months old. I was too wild, and she deserved better. She was an amazing young lady and worthy of being a wife. We decided to co-parent for a little while. That was the best decision for us at that time. I later chose to take on the responsibility as a full-time father. I had my son with me from Monday through Friday every day and Jayln's mother would have him on the weekend. I made this decision because I wanted her to be able to focus and finish school. I did not know at the time how considerate and noble my acts were. Later I realized I was gaining positive grown man's traits. This was one of the most challenging situations in my life. Being a father to a baby alone. Doing all that needs to be done for Jayln. A couple of weeks went by, and I realized something. I did not sign up for this. I swallowed my pride and told my son's mom let's be a family and make this work. I made the mistake of not staying committed to my word. Which was I was going to do right by her. Instead, I lied, played games, and cheated. It turned out to be a big mistake. I lost her for good. I messed up to the point of no return. She was hurt and fed up. Tired of being sick and tired. I was back where I started. A single father learning how to be a man in the process of learning how to be a dad at the same time by trial and error. It was a crucial situation. I knew I had to better my life. I definitely was not going to neglect my son. My plan was not to have a child at such a young age. I promised myself that if I did, I would always be there so they would not grow up wondering where their father was like I did. I was doing my best to make money the legit way. I tried getting a real job. It was difficult because I had a gun charge that I was fighting to beat in court that was holding me back. I would hustle up money by detailing cars, cutting grass, and fixing small home repairs. It was not much, but it kept us afloat. Life was hard at that point and time. Jayln and I were staying with my mother. I was thinking she would help. That did not go as planned. We did not see eye to eye about something serious. Which led to my mother telling me, "You can get out.". I called one of my friends up. Who I know would give Jayln and I a place we could live and less chaos to deal with. It was going well for the first two months. I found myself a construction job, learning how to build houses. Things started looking up. Until one day my friend says, "Now you got your job. I think it is time for you to go now. My lady cannot walk around the house naked with Jayln and you living here.". Jayln and I had no other place to go. I packed Jayln and I possessions and rented out the nearest Motel. Good thing it was time for Jayln's mother to take Jayln. I really needed a second to clear my thoughts. I did not have the money to cover a motel day by day. I am having a conversation with God at this point. Being down to my last few hundred bucks and my construction job ended. My first thought was, I have to get back to the streets and make it happen. Then my phone rang. It was a distant cousin I barely talked to. Calling to check on me. I let him know exactly what was going on. He said, "No worries. Jayln and you can stay with me until you get on your feet.". This was one of the most amazing moments in my life where God moved when I needed him to the most. I am forever grateful that God changed my mindset and my life. The power of positive tongue-speaking affirmations into the universe over your life, is as important as you reaching your destination. Jayln and I were now living on a college compass. Jayln was a little older to the point he was crawling all over the place. Seeing Jayln enjoying himself and his adorable little laughs, kept me aiming to stay positive and motivated. One day my cousin gave me his lunch card to the cafeteria. I walked in with Jayln strapped to my chest. All eyes in the cafeteria were on the young man with the baby. This was one weird moment. In my head I am like, aww shit they know I do not go here. I am about to get kicked out. The cafeteria lady says, " Young man what are you doing with that baby?". I said, "Mam, we just here trying to get something to eat. I do not go here, but my family is looking out for me.". The cafeteria lady says, "Young man, your son and you can eat here everyday. Do not worry about nothing. Here goes some food for y'all. My heart immediately dropped. I have never had things happen for me this way. I was use to having to make things happen. The more spiritual awareness I gained, the more I knew putting God first, having love, faith, hope, and believing will automatically open doors you do not have to touch. Remember, being a good father is a constant journey. Not a destination. Consistently working on improving your relationship with your children and adapting your approach as they grow and change comes with the mastering of balancing fatherhood.

Chapter 3
Balancing Fatherhood

Co-parenting at the beginning was challenging due to our youth and lack of proper communication. Overall, we put our differences aside and came to an agreement that we would split the responsibility with Jayln Fifty-fifty. We did what worked best for us. We both were prosperous. Jayln's mother finished school and went for a CNA license, and I found time to go to trade school to become a building maintenance technician. A few years went by. Now, Jayln is a toddler running around healthy and talking. My cousin, Jayln and I were living in a town house my cousin and I went half and half on. My cousin did not have any children. We were the same age, but I am more mature than my cousin is. One thing about the streets. It is not like you can just walk away from that style of living overnight. Especially when you are good at selling a product. I did what was necessary at the moment and time, to provide and sustain what I had. On the days I did not have Jayln. My cousin and I would throw big cook-outs with some gorgeous young ladies. Who wanted to drink and get loose. It was like I was stuck in a loop of a turn up lifestyle, because the party life has been a major part of my life from childhood till this specific time in my life. The moment I would get Jayln, the turn up was still going on, but I would go into father mode and start separating myself from the activities. I would direct my attention to teaching Jayln how to write letters, say his numbers and alphabet, how to draw, and understand a man's role. We went skating and to the parks just to keep him smiling, laughing, and enjoying life. Jayln enjoying life was enough for me. I started to feel like I was a kid again. Doing all the things I could not when I was his age. At that time frame, I was twenty-two years old and still learning about life and the man I was aiming to become. I was barely working, still surviving the best way I know how. Making moves in the streets and my side hustles. I made sure nothing I did outside of home interfered with me taking care of Jayln. I did not know exactly when, but I knew I was going to have to sit down and make a choice. To live righteously and take care of Jayln or live wicked and destroy Jayln and my life. One late afternoon my cousin comes into the house angry and upset. I asked him what was going on. Turns out he got fired. Rent is due. I only have half of the rent to pay, and he has nothing at all to contribute. There is no legitimate way I can get the rest of the money up to pay the rent. Our young, misguided minds started to develop a plan to rob a drug dealer. (The lack of positive male role models creates this type of mindset.) We masterminded how we were going to do it. We found one more person to join in. All we needed him to do was grab the cash. While my cousin subdues the drug dealer, my friend grabs the cash,

I would be in the car waiting for a clean get away after both of them were back in the car. We made the move about three in the a.m. in the morning. All of us in all black attire with all black masks heading to the drug dealer's location. Not really considering the consequences of my actions and how this could ruin my life. My only thought was to get this cash to maintain what we have. I am behind the wheel and all of us are high and pumped up about robbing the drug dealer. It was just our luck to ride past a shopping center with the alarm going off crazy loud plus three sheriffs in the parking lot watching the only car on the road going the speed limit passing by. Immediately after we passed them, one of the sheriffs jumps out behind us and turns the lights on. It was not my car, so I calmly asked my cousin, "What do you want to do? I can stop, but we got to make a break for it because we got guns in the car.". My cousin thought about it for a few seconds. By this time, they are yelling, "Pull the car over!" over the intercom. My cousin said, "Let's go!", So I floored it. Instantly speeding off from the sheriff. Everyone was excited. For some reason we all felt an exhilarating rush as soon as I accelerated. I do not know how. I was either very experienced in driving unknowingly or God was covering us through this high-speed chase. While there is more than one sheriff chasing me. I am talking to my cousin and friend letting them know what I am about to do before I do it. Thinking, I have to shake these guys off. We are going about a hundred miles per hour. One sheriff is on the left of us and the other one on the right side of us. Both flashing their lights yelling, "Stop the car!". My instincts were superior. I slammed on the brakes coming up on a neighborhood. Once I saw the sheriffs zoom past me with their flashing lights. I mashed the gas, turning immediately into the neighborhood. Things have been looking good so far. We were laughing, like it was a joke. The whole time our life was on the line. I am jumping speed bumps with all four tires off the ground. That is how fast I was going. Coming up to the exit point I seen two police cars blocking the way out. I told them, "Get ready! We have to get out and run.". Seeing a very long driveway to my left I told them, "Get ready!". I turned in. Everyone hopped out and ran as fast as we could. I jumped over a few fences and ran through a few cuts. I finally made it close to home. My cousin did not. I figured he got caught from all the running. Playing it safe, I did not go straight home. Using my intelligence, I went next door to case out our town house. God was with me for sure. Fifteen minutes later the police were wrapped around the block like we committed a murder. I saw my cousin face down in handcuffs. Reality started to set in. I realized I got Jayln coming in a few days and tonight, I could have been taken away from him. Positive role models create and order for young boys which helps them develop into young men. As time goes by, I am still learning how to become the man I need to be for my family. As a parent, balancing your responsibilities with your children and other aspects of your life can be challenging. Here are some tips that may help. First tip, prioritize by making a list of your responsibilities in order of operations. For example, if spending time with your children is your top priority, then schedule your work and other commitments around the time you have set for your children. Second tip, Plan ahead of time. Plan your time in advance. Stick to your schedule as much as possible.

This will help avoid last-minute conflicts that can disrupt your time with your children. Third tip, Be present. When you are with your children, be fully present and engaged. Put away distractions like your phone or laptop and focus on enjoying your time with your kids. Fourth tip, communicate with your parents and family members about your responsibilities. Speak on how they can support you in your efforts to be a good parent. Fifth tip, take care of yourself. Make sure to take care of your own needs physically and mentally. Taking care of yourself will also help you be more present and engaged with your children when you are with them. Finding balance is an ongoing process. It is okay to make adjustments over time. Prioritizing your responsibilities, planning ahead, being present, communicating, and taking care of yourself you can successfully balance fatherhood through all aspects of your life, but never forget you will have to make a fathers sacrifice.

Chapter 4
Fathers Sacrifice

Time waits for no man. Jayln is now five years old, and I am 25 years old currently. I have learned a lot over the years and have been through a lot as well. This journey of learning to become a man and or father at the same time is no easy task. I have a slight idea, but no real clue on what a real man and or father is. One thing I do know for sure is, I am tired of struggling and having enough just to get by. Always having to figure out a way to sustain by hustling to provide doing what is necessary to maintain. The arrangements Jayln's mother and had at the time are still the same. Fifty-fifty possession but flexible. Unless Jayln's mother had something to do. We would communicate and figure it out from there and it was the same way vice versa. I had no transportation at the time. I would walk everywhere. I started to feel like I was not being productive with my time. Which then led to me getting back into school for carpentry level two at Durham Tech Community College. I would walk to school every day and still end up with perfect attendance. My determination to accomplish something Jayln and I could both be proud of gave me hope and drive to fulfill my desire of giving Jayln a better life. Helping him understand that as long as you put your mind to it. You can do it. In order to get it through to him I knew I would have to lead by example. As I was walking to school something random happened. An older man working on cars at a body shop yelled to me, "Keep your head up young man!". My reply to older man was, "It is always up. I am just focused.". My response shocked him. I asked the older gentleman what his name was. "Pastor Alfred.", he replied. I responded back saying, "Nice to meet you. I am Saquan.". The conversation went from why I see you walking so much? To me telling him about school and that I was about to graduate. Pastor Alfred was happy to hear that. Pastor Alfred tells me afterward, "Young man, come to my church this Sunday.". I brushed Pastor Alfred offer off because I was not brought up in a church. Even though my mother used to say, "Pray and speak to God.". We did not go to church. Finally, the day comes for me to walk the stage for graduation. I am very proud of myself for seeing it all the way through. I finished school, but I still had to sell weed and side hustle for the time being. I was able to cover up the illegal traffic by having cook-outs. Making it look like family gatherings. At that time, I was living with my older female cousin and her children. My cousin had one boy and one girl. They were about four years older than Jayln. Every week there was a house party or cookout. Soon as the kids were in bed and sleeping it was time to turn up. The party or cookout would be packed all the time. Randomly, one night. Packed as usual. My neighbors called the police, I believe for being too loud. The police did not come to the door because my cousin's house was fenced in. I had a lot of drugs in the house and a firearm. I had to come up with a plan to get rid of them. I sent my only white lady friend that was in the house outside to talk to them hoping that she would be able to calm the police down and they would give us a warning and tell us turn the music down and leave. It was too much of a risk for everyone if the police came in. So, my white friend and her friend did go out to speak with the officers, but her friend was drunk. There were people outside already talking to the officers and one of them were being racist toward one of the black guys and my white friend's friend went off mouthing the racist cop because she was offended by the comment being used by the cop. The situation took a turn for the worst. It was getting very loud outside to the point where people that were on the inside started to go outside curious about what was going on. I run to the back and make sure the drugs and gun was hidden good and make sure that the kids were still sleeping. All of a sudden, I hear everyone yelling, "Stop!". Then the cop slammed her to the ground. We were trying to help her, but the other officers blocked us out. I knew then, I had to take control over the setting for the entire home because I am the only man of the household. That situation was so nerve wrecking we all began to protest and march in front of the police station for justice. Comes to find out that the cop was known for aggressive behavior and ended up getting suspended but no serious punishment. Witnessing racism in person makes you view life in a life altering way. We fought for a long time. Protesting and marching every day until it died down and everyone stop fighting for the cause. My cousin and I sat down and had a deep conversation about our future. I told my cousin, "Let's do better. Let's live right.". I got rid of drinking and partying. We started taking the kids to church. I always had the desire to do better. I just never found it in me to take the first step. I guess there is a first for everything. Listening to the word of God felt amazing and gave me a desire and motivation to strive for better. It was a force over me I felt like never before. All of us started praying together as a family and eating healthier as well. I slowed down selling weed and ended up with a catering job for the entire year. Then I was able to quit because I was offered a higher paying job. Things were really starting to look up for us. Seeing God move in my life, in such a mighty way gave me understanding that there is truly a higher power. I was verily seeing by faith and not by sight. I began to pray a lot more. The more I got in tune with God the more I discovered who I am and my purpose on this earth. Also, understanding that life is going to come with trials, tribulations, and testing as I live, learn, and grow. Yes, I slowed down dealing, but it was not over yet. One night I am making a play. A few friends and I got pulled by the police. I just knew I was going to jail because what I had tucked on me. The police told us to get out of the car. Searched the car. I did not find anything. While the police searched the car, I did not have the time to throw the drugs off me. Plus, the police had lights all over the place. So, I prayed to God the police would not find anything before I was searched. With my hands up and eyes closed the police began to search. "Clean. Let them go.". Says the officer. I could not believe it but could believe at the same time that they let us go because this was not the first time something extraordinary had happened to me. Scraping and saving every penny I had I was able to finally get Jayln and I a place where we could call home again. Jayln had his own room and I had mine. Just the two of us. Jayln and I love spending time with each other one on one. I loved teaching him things like playing basketball and swimming. Jayln and I had an awesome time bonding. Together, Jayln and I life was becoming a bit more structured. I was so proud of myself for continuing through the midst of it all. Going to church every other Sunday to get a better understanding of God and my purpose for me in the world became more consistent. A father may sacrifice many things in order to support and provide for his family, including his personal time, hobbies, and interest. Fathers may work long hours or take on additional jobs to ensure that his children have the resources and basic necessities that his children needs to thrive. A father may also give up his own desires or dreams in order to put his family first. Ultimately, a father's sacrifice is a selfless act of love and devotion to his family. Conversations or knowledge and understanding of what happens before fatherhood, the beginning of fatherhood, balancing father hood, and father sacrifices is somethings that should be shared from generation to generation, father to father.

Chapter 5
Father To Father

Thanking God every day for allowing me to maintain a home. Jayln is steady growing a prospering. It is going well. Been a few years now and I realize that the older a child gets there is a new level of parenting you enter in. Jayln is in school learning the ropes of a young black boy as well as being bullied and learning to defend himself. Started teaching him how to protect himself through the art of boxing techniques. Jayln deals well with his life overall and I am proud of the young man he is becoming. Unexpectedly, I ended up bumping into my father at the mall doing some shopping. My father was happy to see me, but there has been so much time that has passed by since we last talked. It really was not a big deal to me to see him. I let him know that he was a grandfather now and that Jayln was seven years old now. My dad gave me respect for taking care of my responsibility as a man and taking care of what was mine. My father respected that. My pops and I exchanged numbers and made plans to have a sit down and catch up. During that time frame I was working for a company called Will Scott repairing modular space units as a lead technician in charge of running gear. Weekends were flexible for me. So, my dad and I would catch up, talk business, and make plans for the future. Pops and I started to create a bond for the first time. It seemed to be the beginning of something good. I was truly at peace with his absence in my life and was moving forward. Felt liberating! That is the best word to describe freedom, like a weight had been lifted of hurt and pain off my soul. I was proud of myself for growing into a man and a father no matter what the circumstances were. It demonstrates character and honor and for that, I thank God for adding those attributes to me. My dad called me up one day and invited me over for dinner with him and his lady. I stopped by. We had good conversations about business and searching for properties to fix and flip. Steady speaking of self-sufficiency guesses. I got that naturally from my father, because I was always an entrepreneur. Nothing seemed out of the ordinary. So, I left and expected to hear from him later on my birthday, February the first. I did not expect to receive a call on February the tenth. That call I got while I was at work changed my life. My dad was in the hospital due to a massive heart attack. Instantly I started praying, not knowing how serious it really was. I left with my work gear on. Heading to the hospital talking to God. Trying to stay in a positive head space. I am saying to myself, "Dads fine. Pops a soldier. He was a marine. Pops can beat this. I am going to walk in, and everything is going to be ok.". I do not know anything about the heart attack besides what the hospital told me. My thought was I am going to walk in and see my dad laying in a hospital bed watching tv. What I saw was the complete opposite of that. I have never seen what I saw. Not even on tv. There were so many tubes in his chest and mouth, I was in total shock. My heart dropped. I broke down in tears. I wiped them constantly trying to be strong for him, but it was unbearable. My heart was hurt. I mean crushed. Praying to God while crying telling God to heal him. No one deserves to suffer the way my father did, in the midst of the machines keeping him alive while having seizures too. I was there all night by his side. Being as strong as I could be. My mother came to support my father and I. Outside of my father's girlfriend he had no family except a sister and her kids whom I did not know. It was to the point now where only the machines are keeping him alive. Pops were having too many seizures back-to-back. Doctors were telling me it is my decision to pull the plug, but I was in shock and was not in any condition or mindset to rush to make a decision like this one. Even though he was not responsive, I feel in my heart he still heard me. I held his hand and told him, "I love you no matter what and I forgive you.". A tear fell down from his left eye. I walked out head down in shambles. All I kept thinking was this cannot be happening right now, but it was, and I was not prepared. I do not even like funerals, but now I have to plan one. My dad died February the thirteenth. In the little time we had together I learned a lot from him. I was so unstable emotionally, because my father was absent throughout my life for a long time. What really hit me the most was me walking into his job letting his employees know. Walking into banks informing them as well. I felt like it was weighing on me because I was the one who had to inform everyone. With the help of my father's girlfriend and my mother it was a blessing, everything was set. Pastor Alfred and his wife shared a word for his passing. One thing I learned for sure is prepare for the unexpected as much as you can. You never know when it is your time to go to the after-life. There are so many questions I did not get to ask my father and I will never get the chance to. All I know now is that in Jayln's life and any other child I may have life, I need to do, explain, and know a father's role.

Chapter 6
Fathers Role

The passing of my father, a man I barely knew helped mold me into the man I am today. It is no easy task to deal with the death of a parent. The way I felt was indescribable. So many mixed emotions I experienced that I could not understand. Why at the time my father and I were rebinding, my dad had to go. This experience made me understand that time waits on no one, and as a father if you do not prepare your kids for life without you, you have failed as a parent. My dad had nothing in place. No will. No life insurance policy. So, I had to cover his funeral. Which is not an issue. It educated me on how to prepare my children for my passing. A year passed by. I was so used to my dad not being around, that my dad passing away slipped my mind. I saw a car riding by that was similar to the car he owned one day, and I ended up riding past that car and blew the horn thinking it was him. Shortly after I remember thinking damn, pop is gone. The thought broke me down for a second. There are so many unanswered questions that I will never get to ask. Everything happens for a reason, because this tragic situation elevated my mind, body, soul, and spirituality. I started studying natural ways to heal the body with food and herbs. The more I learned, I passed down the knowledge to Jayln. This experience made me think a lot clearer as far as how I prepared Jayln and myself to be able to survive without me. Truth be told everyone has a start date and a finish date. Good thing is Jayln is intrigued with food and cooking which is a great start. I conversate with God a lot more. Asking God for guidance and order. I am nowhere near perfect, but I am taking all the necessary steps to become all I can be. While in the process, I am encouraging Jayln to do the same. I taught him an affirmation, something that he will never forget and maybe one day pass it down to his children. Quoting the affirmation, (I would ask, "What are you?". Jayln replies, "A man.". Then I would ask, "What else?". Jayln replies, "A king.". I ask, "What does a man supposed to do?". Jayln replies, "Take care of his family.". I ask, "What else?". Jayln replies, "Protect his family." I ask, "What is the most important thing to life?". Jayln replies, "Health". I ask, "What is the kingdom standard for a strong family?". Jayln replies, "Through wisdom a house is built. Through understanding it is established.".). This affirmation we have been going over for years. No matter where we are or where Jayln and I are going. We could be on the highway go so where and I would turn the music down and ask him those questions, just so he can remember his role in life. It is to the point where it is embedded into his soul taking his journey doing the role of a man or father. I am proud of the young man Jayln is becoming. The more I learn about life while striving to become a better man, I pass wisdom down to Jayln. I feel it is very important to teach self-defense, spiritual awareness, and self-discipline. These tools are highly important when it comes to growth and development. Practicing these tactics helps with self-control and critical decision making in the midst of chaos. Learning more about assets and liability, knowing the value of a dollar, and how to generate your own income is something I will always strive for with the ultimate goal of becoming self-sufficient. As I live and learn I am going to teach my children the best I can to help them on their journey. I have noticed as Jayln gets older facing life challenges it motivates Jayln and I to go harder. The best advice I could give to any upcoming father is do not worry about what anyone thinks. The lion does not concern himself with the thoughts of food or prey. Attack the world as if you have nothing to lose. Never give up on your goals and your dreams. To display to your children a powerful trait of faith and consistency. Being in an environment. Living in a survival state of mind. You do not consider your kids or your own diet. This is very important to ensure their strength and your strength for the future. The more natural the better. Having more home cooked meals than fast food is always the best choice. A father's role is one of the most important roles on the planet passed down from the creator of all. God never called himself a mother. God gave man his title father, to carry. Carrying Gods title comes with great responsibility. You need to understand his character and nature. A father is the source and sustainer of his creations or things. The father is the foundation of his family. A family built without a solid foundation will fall. Gain wisdom from other people's mistakes and have the willingness to learn from all. Forgiveness is a major key principle you should do to truly grow and operate in divine love. A father's love is the foundation upon which a child's future is built. In order to provide the type of love necessary to help your child build a positive future. You would have to love yourself first and appreciate yourself more often. The level of devotion toward your children's well-being will consume the majority of your time. Once you find the right balance and your scheduling permits. Take that time out to regroup. Making time for yourself will always help keep you grounded. Time management is important. Write down the specific tasks for yourself along with the babies sleeping time, play time, and learning time. From my experience, I recommend that you take a nap when the baby takes one. Until his or her sleeping pattern is where you need it to be. It is not what we leave behind for our children. It is what we instill in our children that truly makes a difference in their role in the world. Faith is crucial. Seeing what most people consider impossible becomes possible for you, because the amount of faith you have on earth allows you to fulfill your purpose through all the odds that were against you. All praises to the most high for the wisdom and understanding to perceive clearly from the lessons God put in my life and the knowledge to apply what is needed to receive wisdom. The beginning to unlock true wisdom comes by accepting the source of creation.

Chapter 7
The Source Of Creation

Growing up in poverty with the lack of resources is not an excuse for staying in that position. Prayer plus action equals results. Outside of being in a survival state of mind. I had visions of what I wanted my family structure to be for Jayln and possibly future generations. So, everything I knew was thrown to the side and I started re-educating myself on finances and investments to becoming self-sufficient to sustain this generation on to the next. Financial Literature is not taught in school or money management. The unawareness of using credit or how to maintain it and utilize it for your own benefit is another pit fall on the grounds of not knowing. This information was not passed down from my family or my parents. I took it upon myself to do research, take notes, read, ask questions from individuals who have more experience at managing and investments. Obtaining the skill trade of carpentry and general contractor work a master level, based on all the experience I have. I can pass down the knowledge to Jayln by teaching him the basics. What we know about being a father should be passed down from our father. Your father's wisdom should come from the source of creation which is God. What I thought I knew was premature, because most of what I knew came from my environment. A lot of time has passed by, and I realized as I lived, learned, and studied consistently, that striving to become better starts with identifying the problem and making better decisions. Operating at a level of desperation due to insufficient funds not only cripple you as an individual but cripple your children's and your legacy. The best thing to do I learned is to start a cash flow life insurance policy the day your child is born. Something not too high but affordable so no matter what happens you are able to pay for it. With in two to five years, your policy could possibly grow to the point where you can buy a home or invest into a business to give you leverage for higher financial backing. Which could ultimately help you support your family. With all the money you have built up, no credit checks, and no hassles with the banks, this method will become your own bank. I advise, while you are putting your money into the policy for that time period, to develop a concrete plan. Write down all your steps as far as how much and what you are going to invest in and your overall goal for your funds. So, that way you have a business plan in place for your business, before using your funds. Make sure that all your children are covered by the age of eighteen. College would be affordable by being able to borrow from your policy in terms of your payback method. This is how the wealthiest families pass down wealth to the next generation. When you are ready, open a trust fund to protect all the family's assets. I recommend you get the book, "What Would The Rockafella Do?". Filled with all this wisdom of setting the next generation up for success. Break the generational curse of being born in poverty. Let it end with you. Financial freedom should be your ultimate goal as a father that gives your children the opportunity to accomplish their purpose in life. Also instilling values will help the children navigate through their challenges with a level of confidence of making it through no matter what trait transforms into faith. No religious advice, but acknowledgement of a higher power. A source of creation. The creator of all things. Gods' spiritual development will bring balance in your life. Remember, nothing is permanent. Everything has a season. In my opinion, certain situations may recur because you missed the lesson that was meant for you to learn during that moment of growth to walk into your next level. I realize that now the older I get the more my awareness increases. Use your job as a steppingstone. It is not a place to settle or get complacent. Just over broke should not be your final destination. Stay positive as possible and always have the bigger picture of where you see your family in your mind. Focus, pray, believe and visualize where you want to be in life. Manifestation law of attraction is rooted in the mind and heart consistency is key. Kings are not born. They are made through trials and tribulations, conquering anything you enter into, walking with the attitude of a lion. There are two types of animals God compared himself to and that is a lion and eagle. Eagle, because there is no other bird that flies at the altitude of an eagle. Lion, because of its attitude and certain level of belief that has to be in place for developing your life's outcome. Prayer and spiritual development with your children are a good way for them to know that their father is connected to the source of all creations, and not just living without the gratitude of being able to wake up and fulfill your purpose. Be thankful daily and ask for your daily bread. Which means everything you need for the day. Gratitude will go a long way with praise and worship, but mainly repeating from the heart. Minimum worry and stress will help situations in life you cannot control, but how you react to those situations, you can. I quote Napoleon Hill, "O Divine Providence, I ask not for more riches but more wisdom with which to make wiser use of the riches you gave me at birth, consisting in the power to control and direct my own mind to whatever ends I might desire.". I incorporated this into my prayer when I learned this affirmation. It is very important to study to show yourself approved. This book is just a step in the right direction of being a good father. It's an ongoing process but remember what you learned here and there will be more to come next time. May God bless you all!

About the Author

SaQuan Minor is a son, a brother, uncle, most important
of them all a father.
Man against all odds prevailed through tribulations
set out to destroy him.
A young man of peace but will defend what is right at all
cost.
Integrity, morals and principles are a part of my life,
wisdom I gathered through trial and error.
Honestly becoming a father wasn't in my sights as a
young boy but there is no greater gift God could give and
that's life.
A second chance to get life right and give the next
offspring what you didn't have growing up.
Consistently striving for elevation in the mind, body and
soul.
There are only 24hours in a day what you do is what you
become.

www.ingramcontent.com/pod-product-compliance
Lightning Source LLC
Chambersburg PA
CBHW071251150726
48001CB00018B/1085